Special thanks to Luana Horry, Eric Wilkerson, and the talented teams at Kaepernick Publishing and Scholastic for helping to bring my story to life. I hope that these pages may inspire and empower young people to live with confidence and strength in all they do. —CK

Dedicated to my parents for always supporting my artistic dreams. To my two biracial children, LMW & MBW, never give up and good luck will find you. To my wife, I wouldn't be where I am without you. Love, EW. Big thanks also to Mari, Kista, Kofi, GF, CM. —EW

Library of Congress Cataloging-in-Publication Data available
ISBN 978-1-338-78962-1

10 9 8 7 6 5 4 3 2 1   22 23 24 25 26

Printed in the U.S.A. 61
First edition, April 2022

The text type was set in Tomarik.
The display type was partially set in Undersong Solid and also hand lettered by Katie Fitch.
The illustrations were created with Adobe Photoshop.
Endpages were illustrated by Leilani Reid and Knysna Reid.
Production was overseen by Jael Fogle.
Manufacturing was overseen by Shannon Rice.
The book was art directed by Katie Fitch.
Editorial: Celia Lee, Andrea Pinkney, Christopher Petrella
Project Management: Lynn Smith, Tony Ng
Advisory: Debra Dorfman, Kerem Ozguz, Nessa Diab

COLIN KAEPERNICK

I COLOR MYSELF DIFFERENT

SCHOLASTIC INC.  KAEPERNICK PUBLISHING

Hey, I'm Colin.

I read books.

I play sports and games.

And I have a lot of fun
with my friends.

I don't know too many kids who look like me, which makes me supercool. 'Cause I'm different, you know?

I have supercool skin,
supercool hair,
and a supercool family.

Sometimes it's not easy, but being one of a kind
sure is amazing. *Somebody* has to do it.

And that somebody is me! But one day, I had to learn that being different takes courage. It happened at school.

"Good morning, class. Today we are going to learn about families," Mrs. Musa said. "Grab a sheet of paper and your art boxes. We'll start by drawing what our families look like."

This is going to be easy, I thought to myself. *I have the best family ever.*

"I'm going to draw my mom, my sister, and our kitty cat, Mr. Noodles," said Sarah.

"Well, I have a HUGE family, with my parents, grandparents, and lots and lots of cousins. I need two papers," joked Eric, my best friend.

I didn't say anything, because drawing is *serious* business.
I had to choose the just-right pencil, just-right paper, and just-right colors. I had to focus!

First, I outlined, scribbled, shaded, erased, and outlined some more.
Then, I laid out all the crayons so I could pick the perfect colors.

Hmmm . . .

Aha!

Got it!

Finished.

Mrs. Musa asked us to show our family portraits to the class, one by one.

I loved seeing how families look different and beautiful in their own ways. I couldn't wait to share mine.

"This is my mom, my dad, my sister, my brother, and my dog, Kiwi. We like to go to the park, eat cookies, and—"

But before I could even finish, Becky blurted out:

"Why are you the only
brown one in your family?!"

Then I heard from the back:

"Why did you color yourself different?"

At first, I froze.
I was surprised. Shocked. Stunned!
I liked being brown and different,
but the questions made me feel bad.

Then I remembered when I had asked my mom the exact same question.

"Mom, why am I the only brown one in our family? Why am I a different color?"

"Honey, some children join families *when* they are born, and others join families *after* they are born. When you were a baby, Colin, we decided to adopt you, and you made our family whole," Mom answered.

"Adopted means . . . different?"

"Adopted means special." Mom smiled. "Being adopted is an *extra-*special way to join a family. Even though we don't share the same skin color, we share the same love. And that's what matters most."

Ever since Mom wrapped me in that warm hug, I knew having brown skin and being adopted made me special.

I have brown eyes, a brown nose, and brown hands . . .

HUEY NEWTON

TONI MORRISON

ANGELA DAVIS

IDA B. WELLS-BARNETT

. . . just like the people who inspire, create, lead, and change the world.

MALCOLM X

MUHAMMAD ALI

TOMMIE SMITH

AUDRE LORDE

JOHN CARLOS

That made it easy for me to unfreeze quickly.
I stood tall, opened my eyes, and said,

"I'm brown.

I color myself different!

I'm me, and
I'm magnificent!"

I said it a little louder so those in the back could hear me.

"I'm brown.

I color myself different!

I'm me, and
I'm magnificent!"

"You *are* magnificent—magnificently brown and magnificently different," affirmed Mrs. Musa.

"Brown is beautiful," added a classmate.
"Brown is the color of my favorite superhero!"

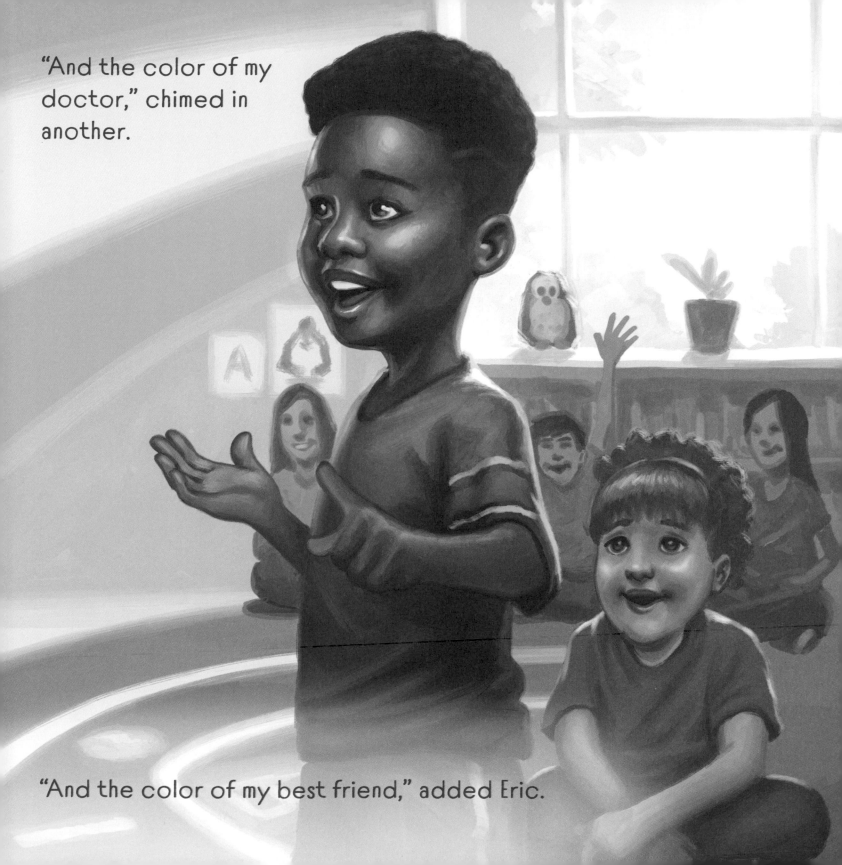

"And the color of my doctor," chimed in another.

"And the color of my best friend," added Eric.

Mrs. Musa smiled and clapped her hands. "Wonderful, my magnificent students!" Then she talked about the ways people and families can be different and full of love.

I love my brown skin and I love my family. I love being different!

As we talked, I snuck a few seconds to add something very special to my family portrait before hanging it up on the wall.

That day, I was proud. I was proud of my brown skin, and I was proud to be me.

It was the day that I colored myself different for all the world to see.

Dear Reader,

The story you just read is true.

The moment I chose to color myself with a brown crayon was a defining moment in my life. I knew that I was different from my family, and I loved myself because of it. I began to understand that my brown skin was connected to my Black identity. It helped me to recognize that the world doesn't always value Blackness. In fact, it can be cruel and unjust, especially for Black people, Indigenous people, and people of color.

Some of you may be thinking young children don't experience racism, but the truth of the matter is that kids as young as age three can develop and express racial biases. It was around this age when I encountered more overt racism and prejudice from my peers . . . but I quickly learned to stand up for—and courageously love—myself in spite of a community telling me that I shouldn't. My sense of self-worth didn't come from me alone, though. I recognize the long line of leaders who came before me and helped me understand what it means to be brave, bold, and Black. In every endeavor—from my KNOW YOUR RIGHTS camps to the letter you're reading right now—I want to empower and encourage young people to love themselves, know their inherent worth, realize their strength, and use their power to change their communities . . . and ultimately the world.

I hope you will join me in this undertaking. It's not always easy to stand up and be who you are, but little by little and person by person, our collective voices and stories will transform the world into a more equitable and just place. Keep being you. You're magnificent.

THE LEADERS FOUND IN THIS BOOK BECAME CHAMPIONS OF FREEDOM BECAUSE THEY DARED TO BE DIFFERENT AND COURAGEOUS.

DR. HUEY P. NEWTON (1942–1989) co-founded the Black Panther Party for Self-Defense in Oakland, California, in 1966 and believed in the power of young people to radically change the world.

DR. ANGELA DAVIS (born 1944) is a prolific writer, professor, and a founding member of Critical Resistance, an organization whose mission is to abolish prisons and police.

IDA B. WELLS-BARNETT (1862–1931) used her courage and talents as an investigative journalist to report on acts of violence against Black people. She also helped to establish the Alpha Suffrage Club, the first voting rights organization for Black women.

TONI MORRISON (1931–2019) authored eleven novels during her lifetime that beautifully celebrate Black joy, hope, and resistance. In 1993, she was awarded the prestigious Nobel Prize for Literature for her work.

MUHAMMAD ALI (1942–2016) used his platform as one of the greatest heavyweight boxing champions of all time to speak out against racial injustice and militarism. For his stance, he was stripped of his boxing title and banned from the sport for three years.

AUDRE LORDE (1934–1992) dedicated her life to centering the voices and literary work of Black women and women of color. As a queer Black feminist writer, Lorde published over fifteen books of poetry and prose, including her well-known *Sister Outsider*.

TOMMIE SMITH (born 1944) and **JOHN CARLOS** (born 1945) are best known for protesting oppression against Black people by raising their black-gloved fists—a symbol of Black Power—at the winner's podium of the 1968 Mexico City Olympics during the playing of "The Star-Spangled Banner." Despite having just won the gold and bronze medals, respectively, for the 200m sprint, they were suspended from the team two days later.

MALCOLM X (1925–1965) was an influential leader of the twentieth-century global Black freedom movement who famously declared that Black people must be respected as human beings "by any means necessary." Malcolm X credited much of his activism to his love of reading. ". . . I could spend the rest of my life reading, just satisfying my curiosity. . . ," he wrote in his autobiography.